Going Buggy!

by Patty Michaels
illustrated by Alison Hawkins

Ready-to-Read

SIMON SPOTLIGHT
An imprint of Simon & Schuster Children's Publishing Division
New York London Toronto Sydney New Delhi
1230 Avenue of the Americas, New York, New York 10020
This Simon Spotlight edition May 2022
Text copyright © 2022 by Simon & Schuster, Inc.
Illustrations copyright © 2022 by Alison Hawkins • Stock photos by iStock
Manufactured in the United States of America 0322 LAK
2 4 6 8 10 9 7 5 3 1
Library of Congress Cataloging-in-Publication Data
Names: Michaels, Patty, author. | Hawkins, Alison, illustrator. Title: Going buggy! / by Patty Michaels ; illustrations by Alison Haw-
kins. Description: New York, New York : Simon Spotlight, [2022] | Series: Super gross | Audience: Ages 5–7 | Audience: Grades K–1
| Summary: "Fly into the astonishing life of bugs in this super fun and super gross book in a new nonfiction Level 2 Ready-to-Read
series about all the grossest things!"— Provided by publisher. Identifiers: LCCN 2021061372 (print) | LCCN 2021061373 (ebook) |
ISBN 9781665913409 (hardcover) | ISBN 9781665913393 (paperback) | ISBN 9781665913416 (ebook) Subjects: LCSH: Insects—
Juvenile literature. Classification: LCC QL467.2 .M53 2022 (print) | LCC QL467.2 (ebook) | DDC 595.—dc23/eng/20211217
LC record available at https://lccn.loc.gov/2021061372 | LC ebook record available at https://lccn.loc.gov/2021061373

Glossary

abdomen: the part of the body that contains the stomach and intestines.

antennae: movable body parts that occur in pairs on the heads of insects.

arachnids: members of the arthropod group of animals. They include spiders, scorpions, ticks, and mites.

bug: any type of insect, arachnid, or myriapod.

carnivores: animals that eat mostly meat.

Goliath: something that is very large.

invertebrate: a living thing without a backbone.

larvae: animals in an early stage of development that differ greatly in appearance from their adult stage.

myriapod: arthropods with a body made up of numerous similar segments. Millipedes and centipedes are myriapods.

specialty: something for which a person is well known.

species: a specific kind of living organism.

thorax: the part of the body between the head and the abdomen.

Note to readers: Some of these words may have more than one definition. The definitions above match how these words are used in this book.

Contents

Chapter 1:
The Lowdown on Bugs

Hello! My name is Dr. Ick.
It's a delightful name, isn't it?
Bugs are my **specialty**
(say: SPEH-shul-tea).
I just love a good bug!
The creepier and
the crawlier, the better!

This is my good friend, Sam.

He is not a fan of bugs.

Did you know that there are millions of **species** (say: SPEE-shees) of insects?

That's too many insects for one book.
But in this book you will read about some of the biggest, smallest, and creepiest ones!

Some insects live in
large groups.
They each have a job to do.
Some are considered workers,
while others are crowned
the QUEEN!

So, what exactly is an insect?
Insects are **invertebrates**
(say: in-VER-ta-brates).
All insects have three body parts:
a head, a **thorax** (say: THOR-ax),
and an **abdomen** (say: AB-do-men).
The bugs in this book are
all insects.

The more general term "bug" can include insects as well as **arachnids** (say: ah-RACK-nids), like spiders and scorpions, and **myriapods** (say: MEER-ee-ah-pods), like centipedes and millipedes.

So, you can say all insects are bugs, but not all bugs are insects!

Most insects have six legs. They also have **antennae** (say: an-TEN-ee).

Wow! If I had six legs, I could run really fast!

Insects live all over the world in many different environments (say: en-VI-ron-ments).

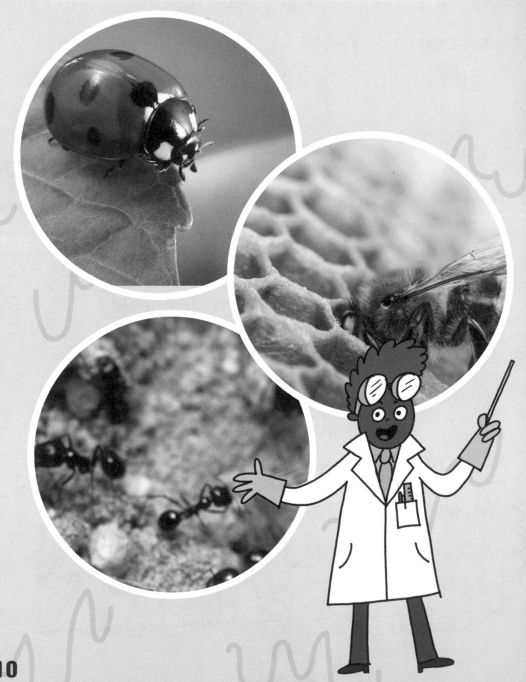

But there are only three species of insects that live in Antarctica (say: Ant-ARK-ti-ka).
One of them is a tiny fly called the *Belgica* (say: BELL-jih-ka) *antarctica*. Its dark purple coloring helps it absorb (say: ub-SORB) sunlight.

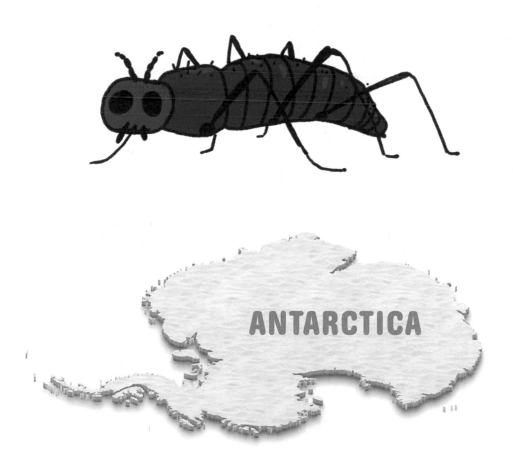

ANTARCTICA

Chapter 2: Flying Bugs, Big and Small!

Now that we know what an insect is, let's talk about some creepy-looking ones that fly!

Meet the scorpion
(say: SCOR-pee-uhn) fly.

It has a black-and-yellow body
and a long beak and tail.
It likes to eat dead bugs
or whatever bug is trapped
in a spiderweb.

Next, I would like to introduce
you to the palmetto (say: pol-MEH-to)
bug. The palmetto bug is another
name for the American cockroach.
It can grow up to two inches long.
That's larger than the size of a quarter!

Next, let's meet the royal **goliath**
(say: go-LIE-eth) beetle.
It is one of the biggest bugs
in the world and can be
as large as a human hand!
Some of its favorite foods
are fruit and tree sap.

Want to learn about
the largest fly in the world?

Say hello to *Gauromydas heros*!
They can be as long as three inches
and like to eat flower nectar.

This is the mango fly.

They live mainly in Africa.
If they bite someone,
they can give them a disease
called African eye worm.
The **larvae** of the eye worm
will grow and live
inside the person's eyeballs!

Check out the thorn bug!
They fly from plant to plant.
Their thorns pierce plant tissue,
allowing them to eat the sap.

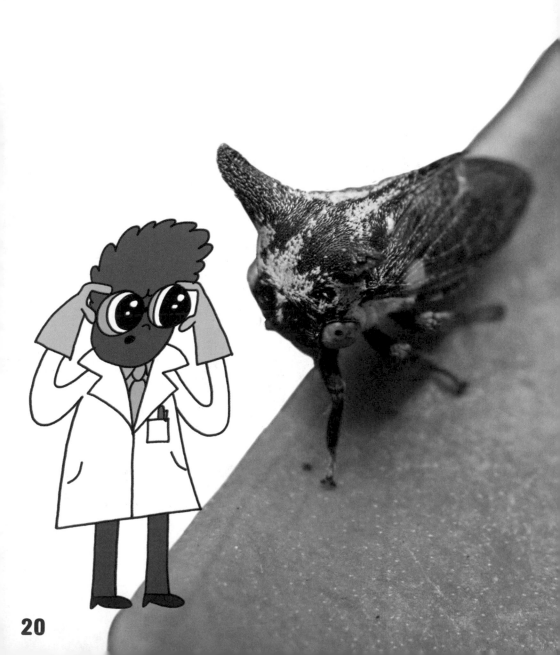

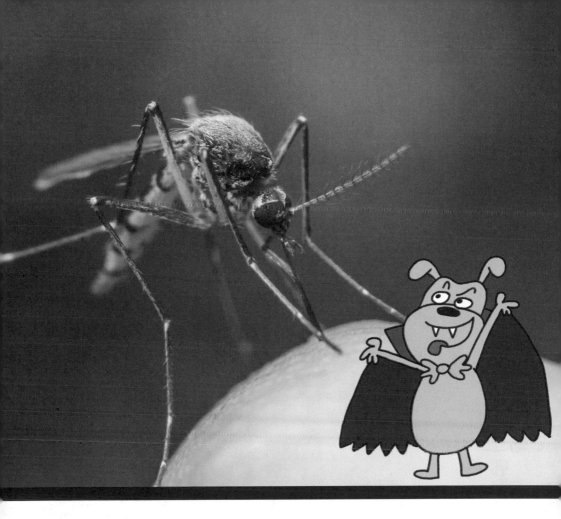

Let's move on to one of the world's
most well-known pests,
the mosquito (say: muh-SKI-toe).
Female mosquitoes bite humans
because they need to drink blood
before they can lay eggs!
Some mosquitoes prefer human blood,
while others prefer animal blood.

Chapter 3: Watch Your Step!

Here are some of the creepiest bugs that crawl on the ground.

First, here is the driver ant.

These ants travel in large groups.

They can march in groups of as many as 22 million at a time!

Driver ants are **carnivores**
(say: CAR-neh-vores)
and mostly eat earthworms.
But they will attack any animal
in their way!

Next, meet the giant wētā
(say: WHEE-ta).
Wētā means "god of ugly things."
They live in New Zealand.

Giant wētā can weigh
up to 2 ½ ounces,
making them one of the
heaviest insects in the world.
(That's about the weight
of a small apple
or a deck of playing cards.)

Sam, check out this insect
called the silverfish!
It mostly lives in people's homes
and eats dead insects, paper,
and even glue!
Silverfish are speedy! They are one
of the fastest insects when they
run back and forth.

This is the camel cricket.
Using their long limbs,
they leap from place to place.
Leaping is the way they scare away
predators (say: PRED-uh-ters).

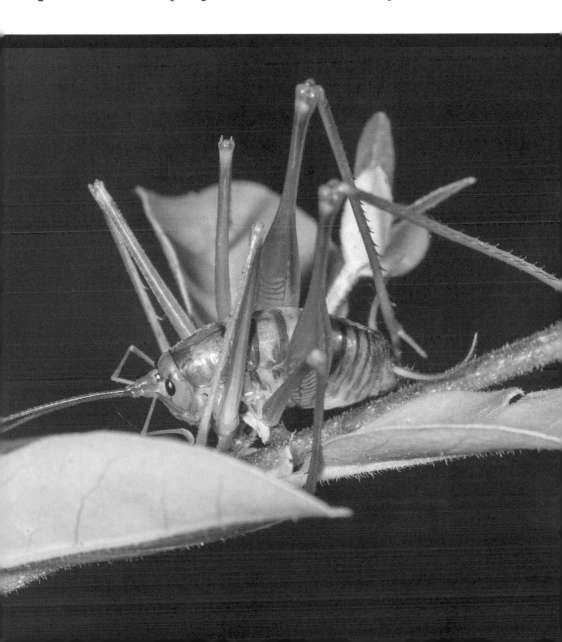

Check out the earwig!
It gets its name because
it was thought to crawl
into people's ears while
they were asleep!

But they don't do that.
They just like to hide
under leaf piles
and mainly eat flowers,
leaves, and other insects.

Guess what?
Did you know that bugs are
very important to our planet?

Bugs help break down
and get rid of waste.
They also pollinate
(say: POL-eh-nate)
flowers, fruits, and vegetables,
helping them to grow.
Let's celebrate our wonderful
buggy friends!

Make Your Own Ant!

Here's an activity where you can make your very own ant!

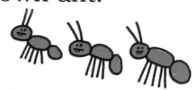

You will need:

- a grown-up to help you
- a cardboard egg carton
- a pair of scissors
- paint and a paintbrush
- 4 pipe cleaners (3 for legs and 1 for antennae)
- a pencil
- a black marker
- glue
- something circular for eyes, such as pieces of dried cereal or googly eyes

Directions:

1. Cut a line of three egg cups from the egg carton. Paint the cups and let them completely dry.
2. Using a sharp pencil, poke one hole on the side of each cup. Then push a pipe cleaner through each hole. These will be the legs of the insect. Bend the legs of the pipe cleaner to make feet!
3. Poke two holes in the top of the very first cup and push a pipe cleaner through the holes. These will be the antennae.
4. Glue the circular items on the front of the carton for eyes. Draw a mouth with your black marker.

Now you have your very own ant!